A Slow Walk with James

A Slow Walk with James

90 Devotional Meditations

Edward B. Allen

Melbourne

A Slow Walk with James:
90 Devotional Meditations
by Edward B. Allen
Copyright © 2018 by Edward B. Allen
All rights reserved worldwide.
Reprinted with revisions, 2020, 2021, 2026.

Published by Edward B. Allen
Melbourne, Florida
Email: edward.allen1949@gmail.com

ISBN: 978-0-9974147-9-0 (paperback)
978-1-7320708-3-7 (standard ebook *.epub)
978-1-7320708-4-4 (Kindle ebook *.mobi)

Cover design by Ken Raney (http://kenraney.com).

To Angie

Contents

Contents

Preface

James, the brother of Jesus,[1] became a leader of the church in Jerusalem. He wrote a general letter to the first-century churches which has been embraced by Christians as part of the Bible ever since. James wrote about a wide variety of topics including genuine faith, wisdom, humility, and prayer. This book is a collection of devotional meditations, slowly walking through the letter from James a few verses at a time. The stories are based on the recollections of actual people and events by friends, family, or myself, unless otherwise indicated. Write your personal thoughts about the passage in the blank space at the bottom of most pages.

The *Christian Standard Bible* (CSB) is quoted as the primary translation of the Bible. It is a modern translation based on the latest evangelical scholarship. Clarifications are in [brackets]. A word referred to as a word is in *italics*. Cross-references to other Scriptures are in the notes. Scripture references consist of book, chapter, verses, and version (if relevant), for example, "James 1:1 (CSB)." All titles and Scripture references are indexed. Male pro-

---

[1]Galatians 1:19 and Mark 6:3.

nouns are sometimes used to indicate a person of either gender.

I thank my many Facebook friends for their encouraging responses to earlier devotional meditations. I am also thankful for the support of my wife, Angie.

E.B.A.

Meditations

1 Servant

> James, a servant of God and of the Lord
> Jesus Christ:
> To the twelve tribes dispersed abroad.
> Greetings.
>
> James 1:1 (CSB)

The Statue of Liberty stands in New York Harbor. Americans treasure the freedom to live as they want. The independent American is an ideal in our culture. Does any American want to voluntarily be a slave? Am I willing to be a slave? Am I willing to give up the freedom to do whatever I want?

Slavery was an integral part of the Roman world. Rather than identifying a human leader, or claiming freedom from restraints, James said he was a servant, a slave. His master was God, and specifically, Jesus. Like a slave in his culture, he was completely submitted to the Lord.

> PRAYER: Lord, I am your servant. I submit myself to you as my master. James is my role model. Amen.

2 Tests

> Consider it a great joy, my brothers and sisters, whenever you experience various trials, because you know that the testing of your faith produces endurance.
>
> James 1:2–3 (CSB)

I faced a big exam in school. I knew the exam would be hard. Would God help me get through this test? When I took the exam, there was one section I had no idea how to answer. That section pulled my grade below passing, but the grading committee passed me anyway, because they decided the question was unfair. God was my defender.

Christians are not exempt from difficulties in life. Every difficulty is a test of faith. One might say, "Will God help me safely get through this?" A trial is an excellent opportunity to see the loving mercy of our omnipotent God.

> PRAYER: Lord, thank you for pulling me through the tough times. I will trust you when the next trial comes. Amen.

PERSONAL THOUGHTS

3 Endurance

> And let endurance have its full effect, so
> that you may be mature and complete,
> lacking nothing.
>
> > James 1:4 (CSB)

We marched everywhere in Army Basic Training.
Sometimes we ran. I was not an athlete, so I feared I
would not pass the Physical Test at the end of training. When the time came, I ran a mile in barely less
than seven and a half minutes. I passed. The training had done its work.

Spiritual trials build faith and endurance for the
next trial. Increasing faith fuels spiritual maturity.
I never want trials, but when one comes along,
I know my own spiritual endurance will become
stronger. The mature believer knows that setbacks
are just temporary, because Jesus reigns over all.

> PRAYER: Lord, help me endure in trials,
> because I know you will provide good
> results. Amen.

PERSONAL THOUGHTS

4 Wisdom

> Now if any of you lacks wisdom, he
> should ask God—who gives to all gen-
> erously and ungrudgingly—and it will
> be given to him.
>
> James 1:5 (CSB)

Software bugs are notoriously hard to find. I worked and worked to find a bug, but came up empty-
handed. After frustrating hours, I remembered this
verse and prayed. The Lord answered and gave me
the insight I needed to find the bug.

When one tries to become wise without God's
wisdom, the result is foolishness. In the Garden
of Eden, eating from the Tree of the Knowledge of
Good and Evil was forbidden,[2] because one should
go to God himself for knowledge and wisdom instead of a tree. The creator of the universe has all
wisdom and knowledge. He wants mankind to become wise, and he is generous with what he knows.

> PRAYER: Lord, I repent for the times I
> ignored you in my quest for wisdom. I
> will be prayerful whenever I'm looking
> for answers. Amen.

---

[2]Genesis 2:15–17.

5   Tossed

> But let him [who lacks wisdom] ask in faith without doubting. For the doubter is like the surging sea, driven and tossed by the wind.
>
> James 1:6 (CSB)

I rode an aircraft carrier across the Atlantic as a contractor for the British Navy. We ran into a nor'easter. The waves were more than thirty feet tall. When I peeked outside, the waves were crashing over the bow onto the flight deck. This huge ship was being tossed about like a toy.

A doubter is like a toy boat, tossed about by every stray thought. "Maybe I can figure this out myself." "Maybe I should ask my friend Joe for the answer." "Will God give me wisdom?" But faith in the Lord is the real answer, because he is generous. Faith keeps me steady.

> PRAYER: Lord, I will trust you to provide the wisdom needed for life's problems, instead of running around in panic. Amen.

PERSONAL THOUGHTS

6 Unstable

[The doubter] should not expect to receive anything from the Lord, being
double-minded and unstable in all his
ways.

James 1:7–8 (CSB)

My Dad had a dock and a rowboat. When I took a
step into the boat, it started rocking. There I was,
one foot on the dock and one foot in the boat. Did
I want to stay on the dock or get into the boat? The
longer I thought about it, the more the boat rocked.

Faith in God is a decision. The longer I think
about this decision, the more unstable life becomes.
Do I want to stay in the world or get in the boat
with Jesus?

PRAYER: Lord, my mind is made up. I
will follow you. Amen.

PERSONAL THOUGHTS

7   Exaltation

> Let the brother of humble circumstances
> boast in his exaltation.
>
> James 1:9 (CSB)

Virgia raised her daughter as a single Mom during the Great Depression (1930s) in small-town Arkansas. She was never rich. In her later years, she worked as a nurse at the state tuberculosis sanatorium. The job provided a room and meals. She said she never felt poor, because God always provided for her.

The Scriptures say God has special compassion for the poor.[3] They seem to find faith more easily than the rich.[4] God promises to exalt the humble in the kingdom of heaven.

> PRAYER: Lord, I will trust you in all my difficult circumstances like Virgia did. Amen.

PERSONAL THOUGHTS

---

[3]Luke 6:20 and Psalm 72:12–14.
[4]Luke 18:24–25.

8 Humiliation

> But let the rich boast in his humiliation because he will pass away like a flower of the field. For the sun rises and, together with the scorching wind, dries up the grass; its flower falls off, and its beautiful appearance perishes. In the same way, the rich person will wither away while pursuing his activities.
>
> James 1:10–11 (CSB)

Saint Francis of Assisi was a man full of faith. He was from a wealthy family, but took a vow of poverty. Americans are rich compared to the rest of the world. As I was beginning my career, I wondered if a vow of poverty like St. Francis' was the key to faith.

James told rich Christians to emphasize humility in their lives, because material wealth is only temporary. As quickly as it comes, it disappears. So I will not be smug and satisfied with a professional salary and an American lifestyle. Money and possessions won't last.

> PRAYER: Lord, help me focus on humility in my relationships. I know riches are just temporary. Amen.

9   Perseverance

Blessed is the one who endures trials, because when he has stood the test he will receive the crown of life that God has promised to those who love him.

James 1:12 (CSB)

Faye lived ten years after cancer was found in her lymph system. As the cancer attacked various areas, her friends had a hard time accepting it. Why didn't God do something? But Faye persevered through the good days and the bad days and through medical treatments with addictive drugs. She kept her smile and love for Jesus through it all. Her crown is waiting for her at the awards ceremony.

A *trial* is a circumstance that tests one's faith. Keeping the faith results in passing the test. Continuing to love God through trying circumstances will be rewarded with an eternal crown.

PRAYER: Lord, give me the strength to pass the tests of my faith and to keep my smile through them all like Faye did. Amen.

PERSONAL THOUGHTS

10   God does not tempt

> No one undergoing a trial should say, "I am being tempted by God," since God is not tempted by evil, and he himself doesn't tempt anyone.
>
> James 1:13 (CSB)

When I had an exam at school, I knew the teacher was not tempting me to lose faith in the benefits of an education. Of course, I took the exam seriously, but the test didn't tempt me to lose faith.

God doesn't tempt anyone to sin. He doesn't tempt anyone to lose faith. Trials and hardship are a natural part of the human condition. God may allow hardship, but his grace is always there to support my perseverance.

> PRAYER: Lord, thank you for your grace to persevere through all my hardships. Amen.

PERSONAL THOUGHTS

11   Temptation

> But each person is tempted when he is
> drawn away and enticed by his own evil
> desire.
>
> James 1:14 (CSB)

That last piece of chocolate cake looks lonely. Maybe it needs fellowship with the other chocolate in my stomach. That last piece of chocolate cake certainly looks sad. Maybe someone should put it out of its misery. There's no one else here who wants that last piece of chocolate cake. I guess I'll have to take care of it.

Where does temptation come from? It comes from me. If I only listen to selfish desires, I will be deceived. If I let the truth of God's Word shine on my desires, I will know the difference between righteousness and evil desires.

> PRAYER: Lord, help me to recognize my
> own selfish desires and to resist temptation. Amen.

PERSONAL THOUGHTS

12 Death

> Then after desire has conceived, it gives
> birth to sin, and when sin is fully grown,
> it gives birth to death.
>
> James 1:15 (CSB)

I planted some small tomato plants in pots on the patio. My desire to be lazy resulted in my forgetting to water them regularly. Consequently, my sin resulted in the death of my tomato plants before they could bear fruit. They were the victims of my sin.

Why do people die? The simple reason is sin.[5] Sin causes death for victims and perpetrators. For example, when the seed of anger is fully expressed, murder happens. Many ills of society can be traced to sinful behavior patterns. Temptation comes from evil desires. Evil desires lead to sin in one's heart. Sin in the heart leads to sin in actions. Sin in the heart and in actions leads to death.

> PRAYER: Lord, I repent of my selfish desires. Please prevent their deadly consequences. Amen.

PERSONAL THOUGHTS

---

[5]Romans 6:23.

13   From above

> Don't be deceived, my dear brothers and
> sisters. Every good and perfect gift is
> from above, coming down from the Fa-
> ther of lights, who does not change like
> shifting shadows.
>
> James 1:16–17 (CSB)

I pulled my car into line at the fast food restaurant
and ordered my meal. When I got to the window,
the cashier said, "The guy in front of you paid for
your meal." He was generous to a stranger.

God is generous. He knows exactly what I need.
Some people think God is an angry judge and a
tight-fisted miser. I won't be fooled by other people's opinions about God.

> PRAYER: Lord, thank you for the many
> good gifts you have given me. Amen.

PERSONAL THOUGHTS

14   God's plan

> By [God's] own choice, he gave us birth
> by the word of truth so that we would
> be a kind of firstfruits of his creatures.
>
> James 1:18 (CSB)

I had a plan for the backyard, shrubs over here and ground cover over there. I put the tiny plants in the ground and watered them every day for a couple of weeks. I said to them, "Live!"

God decided to give mankind freedom from sin. He made a plan. The gospel message that Jesus died and rose from the dead was how I received a spiritual new birth. He said to me, "Live!"

> PRAYER: Lord, thank you for giving me
> eternal life through the gospel message.
> Amen.

PERSONAL THOUGHTS

15 Slow to anger

> My dear brothers and sisters, understand this: Everyone should be quick to listen, slow to speak, and slow to anger, for human anger does not accomplish God's righteousness.
>
> James 1:19–20 (CSB)

When someone cuts me off in traffic, an angry condemnation might come out of my mouth. However, I don't know why that driver did that maneuver. I might be more compassionate if I knew about his situation. My anger won't affect him, but it will hurt me. So, I must forgive promptly.

Thoughtless words stir up arguments. Spoken words are the seeds of anger. Anger is the seed of murder. But carefully listening to another person will stir up compassion instead of anger.

> PRAYER: Lord, help me to recognize when I must listen compassionately, forgo arguments, and forgive. Amen.

PERSONAL THOUGHTS

16   Implanted word

> Therefore, ridding yourselves of all moral filth and the evil that is so prevalent, humbly receive the implanted word, which is able to save your souls.
>
> James 1:21 (CSB)

When I planted a shrub in the backyard, I carefully pulled up all the weeds in the vicinity. I did not want a weed to steal nutrients from my shrub. I dug the right size hole for the roots and I poured some fertilizer in the hole. Then I planted the little shrub. Afterward, I gave it plenty of water, so the soil would embrace the roots.

When the Word of God is planted in my soul, all immorality and selfish desires must be pulled out. They will distract me from God's truth. Humility is like fertilizer for the Word, and the Holy Spirit helps me understand and embrace what the Bible teaches.

> PRAYER: Lord, help me to get rid of distractions and to apply the Word to my life. Amen.

PERSONAL THOUGHTS

17   Merely listening

> But be doers of the word and not hearers only, deceiving yourselves. Because if anyone is a hearer of the word and not a doer, he is like someone looking at his own face in a mirror. For he looks at himself, goes away, and immediately forgets what kind of person he was.
>
> James 1:22–24 (CSB)

Every morning I look at myself in the mirror. I wash my face, brush my teeth, and shave while looking in the mirror. Then, just as James said, I forget what I look like.

Merely listening to a sermon on Sunday doesn't make life better. An hour after church, I've forgotten most of what the preacher said. If I'm reading my Bible out of religious duty, I'm not really benefiting. I probably remember more about Saturday's football game than what I just read.

PRAYER: Lord, I will obey what I learn from my Bible reading. Amen.

PERSONAL THOUGHTS

18   Looking intently

> But the one who looks intently into the
> perfect law of freedom and perseveres in
> it, and is not a forgetful hearer but a doer
> who works—this person will be blessed
> in what he does.
>
> James 1:25 (CSB)

The athlete looked intently at the high bar. He knew
the best technique. He had persevered in his training. He was going to put into action what his coach
had said. He made his run and jumped. It all paid
off as he cleared the bar.

If I will read the Word of God, doing what it
says, I will be blessed. If I persevere in good works,
I will be blessed. If I don't forget what the Word
teaches, I will be blessed.

PRAYER: Lord, help me put into action
what the Bible teaches. Amen.

PERSONAL THOUGHTS

19   Useless religion

> If anyone thinks he is religious without controlling his tongue, his religion is useless and he deceives himself.
>
> James 1:26 (CSB)

My connection to the city water system is controlled by valves on my faucets. If there were no valves, water would run all the time, even when the system gets contaminated. Control valves are necessary.

Controlling one's words is an essential element of pleasing God. For example, I'm not loving my neighbor if my mouth uncontrollably dumps my sinful, negative words on him. Religion is what one does to please God. If I think my religion is okay, but God is displeased by my uncontrolled words, then I am deceived and my religion is useless.

> PRAYER: Lord, my highest goal is to please you. Help me control my words. Amen.

PERSONAL THOUGHTS

20   Pure religion

> Pure and undefiled religion before God
> the Father is this: to look after orphans
> and widows in their distress and to keep
> oneself unstained from the world.
>
> James 1:27 (CSB)

When my parents died about a year apart, I felt like
an orphan. My relatives all lived far away. I may
have looked like a self-sufficient adult, but inside I
needed family nearby. My home Bible study group
embraced me and filled that need in my life.

In the first century, orphans and widows were
often destitute, because they had no family to support
them. This verse applies to caring for anyone
who does not have the support of an extended family.
The Holy Spirit points out who I should look
after, what kind of support I should provide, and
when to provide it.

> PRAYER: Lord, show me how to put
> this pure undefiled religion into practice.
> Amen.

PERSONAL THOUGHTS

21   Favorites

> My brothers and sisters, do not show fa-
> voritism as you hold on to the faith in
> our glorious Lord Jesus Christ.
>
> James 2:1 (CSB)

German chocolate cake is my favorite. Just thinking about it makes my mouth water. If given a choice, it's my pick. However, I'll eat whatever kind of cake you put in front of me.

I naturally like some people. I like to be with them. Some people irritate me. I'd rather avoid them. James says I can't be extra nice to some and ignore others. Because God loves every person, I must give his love to everyone, even the irritating ones.

> PRAYER: Lord, I will love whatever kind of person you put in my path today. Amen.

PERSONAL THOUGHTS

22   Not favoring the rich

> For if someone comes into your meeting wearing a gold ring and dressed in fine clothes, and a poor person dressed in filthy clothes also comes in, if you look with favor on the one wearing the fine clothes and say, "Sit here in a good place," ... haven't you made distinctions among yourselves and become judges with evil thoughts?
>
> James 2:2–4 (CSB)

A well-dressed couple visited church for the first time. When the pastor greeted them, he found out the husband was a professional. From that moment on, the pastor treated them as the most important people in the world. He was thinking, "They might be big financial supporters."

James warned against favoring the rich over the poor. Expensive clothes don't matter to God. An important position in the community doesn't matter. Financial support doesn't matter. God loves everyone the same.

> PRAYER: Lord, I'll be careful to avoid favoring anyone because of social status. Amen.

23   Respect for the poor

> For if someone comes into your meeting wearing a gold ring and dressed in fine clothes, and a poor person dressed in filthy clothes also comes in, … yet you say to the poor person, "Stand over there," or "Sit here on the floor by my footstool," haven't you made distinctions among yourselves and become judges with evil thoughts?
>
> James 2:2–4 (CSB)

The men of the church were having a Saturday breakfast and Bible study. When a homeless man came in looking for a rest room, the men welcomed him, made sure he got a good breakfast, and patiently listened to his stories. They made sure he knew when the next free breakfast would be.

James warned against favoring the rich over the poor. Dirty clothes don't matter to God. Sleeping under a bridge at night doesn't matter. The poor are loved by God and deserve respect like anyone else.

> PRAYER: Lord, I'll be careful to avoid favoritism and follow the good examples I've seen. Amen.

24 Heirs

> Listen, my dear brothers and sisters:
> Didn't God choose the poor in this
> world to be rich in faith and heirs of the
> kingdom that he has promised to those
> who love him?
>
> James 2:5 (CSB)

Virgia lived below the poverty line most of her life. Even though she was not rich, her faith in the Lord was strong and her love for him overflowed.

Jesus said, "Blessed are the poor in spirit," and he promised the kingdom of heaven to them.[6] If I don't have material wealth to lean on, then I must put my faith in the Lord. As my faith grows, my love for the Lord grows. God has promised the eternal kingdom to those who love him.

> PRAYER: Lord, my goal is faith and love
> like Virgia's. Amen.

PERSONAL THOUGHTS

---

[6] Matthew 5:3.

25   Oppressors

> Yet you have dishonored the poor. Don't the rich oppress you and drag you into court?
>
> James 2:6 (CSB)

When the youth pastor proposed an outreach to poor college students, a church board member complained they wouldn't contribute money to the church. He was more interested in recruiting rich church members than in spreading the gospel.

In the first century, everyone knew the rich oppressed the poor. James was surprised that Christians, who were mainly from poor classes,[7] would give honor to a worldly rich visitor and disrespect a poor man. Jesus was compassionate both toward a beggar with leprosy[8] and toward Zacchaeus the rich tax collector.[9]

> PRAYER: Lord, help me treat both rich and poor with compassion like Jesus did. Amen.

PERSONAL THOUGHTS

---

[7] 1 Corinthians 1:26.
[8] Mark 1:40–42.
[9] Luke 19:1–10.

26 Blaspheming

Don't [the rich] blaspheme the good
name that was invoked over you?

James 2:7 (CSB)

When I got to college, I was surprised to hear
students say the name of Jesus Christ so often.
They were from respectable wealthy families. I
was pretty sure they were atheists and didn't know
much about the Bible. Why were they saying the
name of Jesus? Then I realized they were using his
name as curse words.

The poor who have faith deserve to be embraced
as brothers more than wealthy atheists who blaspheme.

PRAYER: Lord, give me compassion for
those who blaspheme your name because they don't know you. Amen.

PERSONAL THOUGHTS

27 Love your neighbor

> Indeed, if you fulfill the royal law pre-
> scribed in the Scripture, "Love your
> neighbor as yourself," you are doing
> well.
>
> James 2:8 (CSB)

Growing up in the South during the segregation era
meant I didn't have any African-American friends.
Even though others may have been prejudiced,
my parents always showed respect to any African-
Americans they met. As a child, this was a powerful example to me.

Jesus said the most important law in the Old
Testament is to love God and the second most important is to love one's neighbor.[10] Love for all
neighbors is the best defense against prejudice and
favoritism.

> PRAYER: Lord, help me love everyone I
> come in contact with and to reject preju-
> dice and favoritism. Amen.

PERSONAL THOUGHTS

---

[10]Matthew 22:36–40.

28   Favoritism

> If, however, you show favoritism, you
> commit sin and are convicted by the law
> as transgressors.
>
> James 2:9 (CSB)

My friend grew up in a small town in Mississippi. As a white teenager in the 1960s, she saw the ugliness of favoritism in her church when a delegation of African-American pastors came to her church to worship on a Sunday. Segregation was the norm at that time, so the ushers asked the delegation to leave. My friend was deeply saddened by the attitude of her church's leaders.

This verse is very plain. Favoritism is sin. There is no loophole. There is no escaping conviction in heaven's court on a technicality. Sin leads to death, but when one repents, the mercy of God is there.

> PRAYER: Lord, I see the ugliness of favoring one type of person over another. Amen.

PERSONAL THOUGHTS

29   Grading on a curve

> For whoever keeps the entire law, and yet stumbles at one point, is guilty of breaking it all.
>
> James 2:10 (CSB)

When I was a student, we all wanted tests to be graded on a curve. If I did better than the next guy, I thought I should pass. The teacher thought I should know what we covered in class to pass.

God doesn't grade on a curve. His standard of righteousness is absolute. One sin makes a person a sinner. All sinners need to be rescued by the mercy of God.

> PRAYER: Lord, thank you for rescuing me, even though I was a lawbreaker. Amen.

PERSONAL THOUGHTS

30 Lawbreaker

> For he who said, "Do not commit adultery," also said, "Do not murder." So if you do not commit adultery, but you murder, you are a lawbreaker.
>
> James 2:11 (CSB)

Oops! I was careless. My grip wasn't tight. The coffee mug hit the floor. How much damage makes me a "cup-breaker"? Was the rim chipped? Was the handle in pieces? Was the whole mug was shattered? Any damage makes me a "cup-breaker."

It doesn't matter which point of God's law of righteousness is disobeyed. The offender is still a lawbreaker. Adultery and murder are both obvious sins, but subtle sins like selfishness and anger also make one a sinner.

> PRAYER: Lord, cleanse my life from all kinds of sin, even socially acceptable sins. Thank you for your forgiveness. Amen.

PERSONAL THOUGHTS

31　The law of freedom

> Speak and act as those who are to be
> judged by the law of freedom.
>
> 　　　　　　　　　　James 2:12 (CSB)

While on a business trip, my coworkers and I had dinner with several from the customer company. My worldly coworkers were busy flattering the manager, but ignoring the workers. They were showing favoritism to the powerful. The workers deserved honor, too, because God loves them all.

　　The gospel sets a person free from the law of sin and death.[11] Because a believer is free, he is able to reject favoritism and treat the worker and the manager the same.

> PRAYER: Lord, I will treat both the powerful and the lowly with love. Amen.

PERSONAL THOUGHTS

---

[11] Romans 8:1–2.

32   Mercy triumphs

> For judgment is without mercy to the
> one who has not shown mercy. Mercy
> triumphs over judgment.
>
> James 2:13 (CSB)

While standing in line at the fast-food burger shop,
I tore out the coupon I needed and gave the rest of
the coupons to the guy next to me. A few minutes
later, he asked me for money. He was a panhandler.
I tried to respond as graciously as I could.

When I extend love to someone instead of dis-
dain, when I love equally instead of showing favoritism, when I forgive the weaknesses of others
instead of criticizing, then "mercy triumphs over
judgment."

> PRAYER: Lord, help me extend your love
> to others, even when I might feel judg-
> mental. Amen.

PERSONAL THOUGHTS

33   Faith without works

What good is it, my brothers and sisters,
if someone claims to have faith but does
not have works?   Can such faith save
him?

James 2:14 (CSB)

I have many friends whose parents took them to
church, who sat in Sunday School, who were bap-
tized and said they believed, but they didn't do
what the Bible teaches after growing up.   Their
faith was just cultural and intellectual assent. Some
found genuine faith later as adults.

This verse is the beginning of James' teaching on
genuine faith. The Protestant Reformation reacted
against the practice at that time of just doing things
to earn God's saving mercy. Luther emphasized sal-
vation by faith alone. Some people think this means
intellectual assent to a theological statement. Genuine faith is more than just claiming to agree with
some doctrine. Good works are evidence of faith.

PRAYER: Lord, I will pay attention to
what James taught, so my faith is not
just superficial. Amen.

34   Ingredients

> If a brother or sister is without clothes
> and lacks daily food and one of you says
> to them, "Go in peace, stay warm, and
> be well fed," but you don't give them
> what the body needs, what good is it?
> In the same way faith, if it doesn't have
> works, is dead by itself.
>
> James 2:15–17 (CSB)

I tried to learn to make bread. I mixed a packet of
yeast with water and flour. After a while, the dough
had risen. Yeast, water, and flour are all necessary
ingredients.

James illustrated the hypocrisy of claiming to
have faith while lacking the compassion one should
have toward other disciples. Being a Christian is
not a matter of merely knowing what the Bible says.
It requires obeying the teaching of the Bible as I
grow spiritually. Faith and good works are necessary ingredients of the Christian life.

> PRAYER: Lord, strengthen my faith with
> opportunities for good works you want
> me to do. Amen.

PERSONAL THOUGHTS

35   Showing my faith

> But someone will say, "You have faith, and I have works." Show me your faith without works, and I will show you faith by my works.
>
> James 2:18 (CSB)

The best actor in the senior class was cast as Jesus in the school's production of Godspell. He may have been virtuous on stage, but everyone knew what he was really like off stage.

How can one discern whether someone else has faith? By his good works. A relationship with Jesus fills a believer's heart. Good works flow out of the heart. Trying to be good by will power eventually fails in an unguarded moment. The true motivation of my heart always shows itself when the performance is over.

> PRAYER: Lord, I will focus on my relationship with you, so good works will naturally flow from my faith in you. Amen.

PERSONAL THOUGHTS

36   Believing God exists

> You believe that God is one. Good! Even
> the demons believe—and they shudder.
>
> James 2:19 (CSB)

My friend lived down the hall in the college dorm.
We liked to discuss religion late into the night. I
carefully explained the gospel to him, but he clung
to his own intellectual ideas.

Many people say they believe the God of the
Bible exists. That is a good starting point. However, their actions say they are ignoring him, ignoring his mercy, and ignoring his justice. Demons
know God exists, and they know he will condemn
them in the end. People who refuse God's mercy
and align themselves with demons will join them
in the end. Just acknowledging God exists is not
genuine faith.

> PRAYER: Lord, genuine faith in you is
> my goal. Amen.

PERSONAL THOUGHTS

37   Useless faith

> Senseless person!   Are you willing to learn that faith without works is useless?
>
> James 2:20 (CSB)

I try to avoid debating theology and doctrine. Too often, debating damages love for one another. But if I must, I'll go to the Bible for principles and examples, being careful not to twist the Scriptures.

If one is willing to learn, examples of righteous people who had both faith and works are throughout the Bible. The one who claims works don't matter is foolish, misunderstanding the dynamic relationship between faith and good deeds. I am learning this by experiencing it.

PRAYER: Lord, let my faith in you to be obvious through good works. Amen.

PERSONAL THOUGHTS

38   Complete faith

> Wasn't Abraham our father justified by
> works in offering Isaac his son on the
> altar? You see that faith was active to-
> gether with his works, and by works,
> faith was made complete.
>
> James 2:21–22 (CSB)

Alan Shepard was the first American to go into
space. He was well trained. He understood the
technology. He had faith the rocket would safely
get him into space and the capsule would get him
safely back to earth. Climbing into the capsule atop
a barely controlled explosion completed his faith.

Abraham's actions obeying God's instructions
complemented Abraham's faith. Abraham's faith
was completed by his actions.[12] Assent to proposi-
tions and agreement with ideas is incomplete faith.
Obedience in action speaks louder than reciting
Scriptures.

> PRAYER: Lord, help me complete my
> faith with obedience. Amen.

PERSONAL THOUGHTS

---

[12]Genesis 22:1–19.

39 God's friend

> And the Scripture was fulfilled that says, "Abraham believed God, and it was credited to him as righteousness," and he was called God's friend.
>
> James 2:23 (CSB)

Abraham believed God. He demonstrated his faith by his obedience. He believed if he obeyed, life would go well for him. As a result, God gave him righteousness which was necessary to be God's friend.[13]

To have a close friend-to-friend relationship, there can't be an offense between us. I want to be God's friend like Abraham. There can't be any sin in the way. Jesus paid the price for my sin, so I can have righteousness. I will obey God's Word, too.

> PRAYER: Lord, Abraham is my role model. I will obey you like he did. Amen.

PERSONAL THOUGHTS

---

[13]Genesis 15:6.

40 Justified

> You see that a person is justified by
> works and not by faith alone.
>
> James 2:24 (CSB)

My Dad built a sailboat from a kit. The pieces were cut precisely. The instructions were clear. He had faith the instructions were true, so he did not refuse to screw and glue the pieces together.

Justified means God has forgiven my sin and given me righteousness. Abraham believed God. He had faith. He also acted on his faith. He knew God is good and when God told Abraham to do something, he did it.

> PRAYER: Lord, I know you are good and
> true, so I will not refuse to do whatever
> you say. Amen.

PERSONAL THOUGHTS

41 Rahab

In the same way, wasn't Rahab the prostitute also justified by works in receiving the messengers and sending them out by a different route?

James 2:25 (CSB)

Rahab lived in Jericho when Joshua and the Israelites began to conquer Canaan.[14] She hosted the Israelite spies because she knew their God was powerful. Her actions were the logical result of what she knew by faith.

A friend in Malaysia told me people in the West debate whether there is a god. In Asia, people want to know which god is most powerful. Like Rahab, I know the God of Abraham, Joshua, and Jesus is the most powerful. He is the only true God. My obedience is the logical result of what I know by faith.

PRAYER: Lord, I know you are the only true God, so I will obey you. Amen.

PERSONAL THOUGHTS

---

[14]Joshua 2:1–24.

42   Dead faith

> For just as the body without the spirit is dead, so also faith without works is dead.
>
> James 2:26 (CSB)

A person is not alive if the physical body does not have an active spirit in it. Modern medicine measures brain activity. When the brain is completely quiet, the person's spirit is gone. The person is dead, even though machines may be keeping the heart pumping and the lungs breathing.

I can claim to be a Christian. I can sign a statement of faith to join a Christian organization. What I say must match what I do. Otherwise, it is a lie. Good works are necessary for my statement of faith to be alive.

PRAYER: Lord, help me have genuine faith that is alive. Amen.

PERSONAL THOUGHTS

43   Teachers

> Not many should become teachers, my
> brothers, because you know that we will
> receive a stricter judgment.
>
> James 3:1 (CSB)

After working twenty years developing software, I
changed careers to teach software engineering. The
new career was very rewarding, especially when
mentoring students one-on-one.

Teachers can significantly influence their students, so they bear greater responsibility than those
without such access. This principle is especially
true among Christians. Some are called by the Lord
to be teachers and God gives the grace to fulfill that
calling.

> PRAYER: Lord, thank you for giving me
> the grace to be a teacher. I pray you
> will reward those who have taught me.
> Amen.

PERSONAL THOUGHTS

44   Faultless speech

> For we all stumble in many ways. If any-
> one does not stumble in what he says, he
> is mature, able also to control the whole
> body.
>
> James 3:2 (CSB)

Hoof-and-mouth disease is a viral disease which af-
fects cloven-hoof animals, such as cows. It is highly
contagious and is occasionally fatal. Humans are
not susceptible to this disease, but often get "foot-
in-mouth disease," namely, saying something one
should not say. Without realizing it, I can be a
motor-mouth, letting words come out without any
controls.

Even though I may fight temptation in various
areas, keeping my speech clean and pure is the most
difficult. If I can keep my mouth from sinning, it is
easy to keep the rest of my body under control.

> PRAYER: Lord, help me control what I
> say, so I don't stumble. Amen.

PERSONAL THOUGHTS

45 A horse's bit

> Now if we put bits into the mouths of horses so that they obey us, we direct their whole bodies... So too, though the tongue is a small part of the body, it boasts great things.
>
> James 3:3–5 (CSB)

When I rode a horse for the first time, I was amazed that a piece of metal pressing on the horse's tongue made it stop and go. The horse was gentle and took my poor riding skills in stride.

James illustrated the power of the tongue with several examples. Guiding a horse is the first one. The physical tongue is itself a metaphor for all that I speak. Controlling that small thing controls all of one's actions. All that I speak comes from the inner person, the heart. Whatever is in the heart comes from either the sinful nature or the redeemed person.

PRAYER: Lord, cleanse my heart, so my speech is pure. Amen.

PERSONAL THOUGHTS

46   A rudder

> And consider ships: Though very large
> and driven by fierce winds, they are
> guided by a very small rudder wher-
> ever the will of the pilot directs. So too,
> though the tongue is a small part of the
> body, it boasts great things.
>
> James 3:4–5 (CSB)

My Dad and I raced in a small sailboat. Suddenly
he barked the order and pushed the tiller. I had to
be quick to tend my sail and duck my head as the
boom swung across. The boat seemed to turn in-
stantly.

The rudder of a ship is the second illustration of
the power of the tongue. A rudder is small compared to the ship. My tongue is small compared to
my body. Sarcasm is an example of a small thing
said which can wound the victim of a joke. A sar-
castic joke is intended to be entertaining, but ac-
tually is expressing anger and hate. What I say
may seem small compared to my actions, but words
have big consequences.

> PRAYER: Lord, help me to guard what
> I say and especially to avoid sarcasm.
> Amen.

47   A small fire

> Consider how a small fire sets ablaze a large forest.   And the tongue is a fire. The tongue, a world of unrighteousness, is placed among our members. It stains the whole body, sets the course of life on fire, and is itself set on fire by hell.
>
> James 3:5–6 (CSB)

When I was little, I was a pyromaniac. I loved to play with fire. When I became a Boy Scout, I learned about fire safety, but fire was still fascinating. I could stare at a campfire for hours.

The next metaphor for the tongue is a small fire. Like a forest fire, a small word can devastate many around me. Gossip can spread from person to person, defiling many. What I say can pollute my whole life with sin.

> PRAYER: Lord, I repent of spreading gossip and rumors. Help me speak only good words. Amen.

PERSONAL THOUGHTS

48   Untamed

> Every kind of animal, bird, reptile, and fish is tamed and has been tamed by humankind, but no one can tame the tongue. It is a restless evil, full of deadly poison.
>
> James 3:7–8 (CSB)

I was amazed at the variety of creatures for sale at the pet store. My family had a goldfish for a while. We also had cats. I'm not sure a cat is ever tamed. Maybe our cat trained us. Like our cat, the tongue seems like a wild animal.

Actors are trained to speak with carefully planned words in public. In private, they are like the rest of us, saying whatever profane word pops into their heads. Whatever I'm thinking tends to come out of my mouth. My mind and mouth seem to be connected by an unfiltered pipe.

> PRAYER: Lord, purify my thoughts. I also need your filter on the way to my mouth. Amen.

PERSONAL THOUGHTS

49 Blessing and cursing

> With the tongue we bless our Lord and Father, and with it we curse people who are made in God's likeness. Blessing and cursing come out of the same mouth. My brothers and sisters, these things should not be this way.
>
> James 3:9–10 (CSB)

The singing on Sunday was enthusiastic. The business meeting Sunday night was marred by shouting. One faction wanted to fire the pastor and another supported him. Anger and hatred filled the room. Sunday night was a stark contrast to Sunday morning.

James said the same mouth speaks blessing and curses. He asks how can opposites come from the same place? Whatever I speak comes from my heart. Is my heart clean, so sincere blessings flow or is my heart filthy, so curses flow from anger and bitterness? Are my blessings lies? What I speak is evidence of what is within.

> PRAYER: Lord, cleanse my heart, so I will consistently speak sincere blessings. Amen.

50 Sweet and bitter water

> Does a spring pour out sweet and bitter water from the same opening? ...Neither can a saltwater spring yield fresh water.
>
> James 3:11–12 (CSB)

When I was a boy, most wells in central Florida produced "sulfur water." It smelled and tasted like rotten eggs. It may have been safe to drink, but nobody liked it. My Boy-Scout troop made Kool-Aid with it and called it "bug juice." The well water never tasted good, and the bug juice tasted bad, too.

James presented another illustration about blessing and cursing. Good and bad water can't come from the same spring. Like spring water, blessing and cursing should not come from the same opening.

PRAYER: Lord, help me speak refreshing words, not words like bug juice. Amen.

PERSONAL THOUGHTS

51 Figs and olives

> Can a fig tree produce olives, my brothers and sisters, or a grapevine produce figs?
>
> James 3:12 (CSB)

I had a fig tree in my backyard and a black olive tree. The raccoons came night after night to collect the figs that fell to the ground. The black olive tree just produced thorns. It never produced figs.

James presented another illustration about blessing and cursing. Every tree or vine produces only one kind of fruit, as determined by its DNA. My spiritual DNA as a new creature in Christ is designed for blessing people, not cursing them. What I say must be evidence of the fruit of the Spirit in my life.[15]

> PRAYER: Lord, thank you for making me a new creature in Christ. Help more fruit of the Spirit to grow in my life. Amen.

PERSONAL THOUGHTS

---

[15]Galatians 5:22–23.

52   Gentleness

> Who among you is wise and under-
> standing?   By his good conduct he
> should show that his works are done in
> the gentleness that comes from wisdom.
>
> James 3:13 (CSB)

The referee made his call. The football was down just short of the goal line. Half the stadium cheered and half were outraged.

People become outraged over many trivial things, but the wise person is gentle with others. I am resolved to be outraged only over the things God is outraged about. He is grieved that sinners sin. So am I. He recognizes that people make mistakes. So do I. He knows people say things they regret and didn't mean. So do I.

> PRAYER: Lord, help me respond with gentleness when someone sins, makes a mistake, or says something foolish. Amen.

PERSONAL THOUGHTS

53 Envy and ambition

> But if you have bitter envy and selfish ambition in your heart, don't boast and deny the truth.
>
> James 3:14 (CSB)

When I joined the company, information-technology people were part of the accounting department. My ambition was to become the information-technology manager. But when company grew, someone else was promoted instead of me. Envy and ambition are deceptive.

Envy wants to possess what someone else has. Envy does not recognize that God wants to provide everything I need. Ambition wants to do selfish things. Ambition does not recognize that God prepares good works for me to do. Envy and ambition deny the truth about God's love and mercy.

> PRAYER: Lord, I repent of envy and selfish ambition. Your love and mercy are much better than what I can do for myself. Amen.

PERSONAL THOUGHTS

54   Earthly wisdom

> Such wisdom does not come down from above but is earthly, unspiritual, demonic.
>
> James 3:15 (CSB)

To be published, an academic journal article must present something innovative. So, authors often puff up their results to seem very important, hoping to assure publication. They strive to have as many publications as possible in the best journals to support their professional ambitions.

Envy and ambition masquerade as wisdom. They are not godly wisdom which rejoices in truth, but are demonic, rejoicing in sin. If I profess to be wiser than others, envy and ambition are lurking in my thinking.

PRAYER: Lord, I need your power to cleanse my motivations. Amen.

PERSONAL THOUGHTS

55 Disorder

> For where there is envy and selfish am-
> bition, there is disorder and every evil
> practice.
>
> James 3:16 (CSB)

When we moved into the house, I carefully organized the shed. Every tool had its place. As I
worked in the yard and on projects, I just put the
tools and fertilizer anywhere there was an empty
spot. Pretty soon the shed was a mess.

Healthy relationships have courtesy, openness,
brotherly love, and care for one another. Envy and
selfish ambition wreck relationships and sow con-
fusion. Like keeping an organized shed, I will work
to keep my envy and selfishness at bay, so my relationships are godly and well ordered.

PRAYER: Lord, help me exclude envy
and selfishness from my life. Amen.

PERSONAL THOUGHTS

56 Wisdom from above

> But the wisdom from above is first pure,
> then peace-loving, gentle, compliant,
> full of mercy and good fruits, unwaver-
> ing, without pretense.
>
> James 3:17 (CSB)

The world thinks "knowledge is power."[16] Some people go to school for many years to become influential experts. My twenty years in school may have helped me in my profession, but it did not give me wisdom that is pure, peace-loving, gentle, and merciful.

God's wisdom is virtuous. His wisdom is not argumentative, because it is based on truth. Truth banishes favoritism, because God loves all people. Truth banishes hypocrisy and pretense, because God knows who I really am.

> PRAYER: Lord, give me your wisdom, not earthly wisdom. Amen.

PERSONAL THOUGHTS

---

[16]Francis Bacon, *Meditationes Sacrae, De Haeresibus*. Available at http://www.bartleby.com/100/139.39.html (current September 1, 2018).

57   Peace

> And the fruit of righteousness is sown in
> peace by those who cultivate peace.
> James 3:18 (CSB)

In the checkout line at the grocery store, a mom in front of me was trying to put her groceries on the belt while her baby was being fussy. It was easy for me to distract the baby with silly faces and calm words. Mom then finished her checkout in peace.

Peace is a fruit of the Spirit.[17] Spreading the peace of God as I go through my day is a smart strategy. Helping others get through the bumps in the day will result in more fruits of the Spirit in them and in me.

> PRAYER: Lord, show me opportunities
> to share your peace with others. Amen.

PERSONAL THOUGHTS

---

[17]Galatians 5:22–23.

58   Wars

> What is the source of wars and fights
> among you? Don't they come from your
> passions that wage war within you?
>
> James 4:1 (CSB)

A church called a new pastor by a vote of a bare majority. When he started to change the style of worship services, the half who didn't vote for him complained, "It's no longer like we've always done it." They gradually left the church.

Why do Christians fight with each other? Christians seem to argue more with each other than they do with the world. Arguments, name-calling, and struggles for power litter church history, and the histories of many local congregations.

> PRAYER: Lord, make me a peacemaker
> who calls the brothers back to simple
> love for one another. Amen.

PERSONAL THOUGHTS

59   Do not have

You desire and do not have. You murder and covet and cannot obtain. You fight and wage war.

James 4:2 (CSB)

The loss of some parking spots at the university precipitated a crisis, a flurry of memos, and angry meetings. University people are notorious for being argumentative.

James warned his Christian readers about ungodly behavior. Christians today fall into the same worldly patterns. Ungodly desires, hatred, envy, and fighting are reasons people lack what they desire.

PRAYER: Lord, I will not follow the bad examples of anger, envy, and fighting which James warned about. Amen.

PERSONAL THOUGHTS

60   Did not ask

You do not have because you do not ask.

James 4:2 (CSB)

When I came in from a hot afternoon of playing in the yard, I knew there were some popsicles in the freezer. All I had to do to get one was to ask Mom.

If I assume I must earn everything I want, I will miss out on the generosity of the heavenly Father. Jesus said to ask, seek, and knock, because the Father wants to give good gifts to his children.[18] It is arrogant to think I can get everything I want by my own efforts.

PRAYER: Lord, when I need something, I will come to you first. Amen.

PERSONAL THOUGHTS

---

[18]Matthew 7:7–11.

61   Wrong motives

> You ask and don't receive because you ask with wrong motives, so that you may spend it on your pleasures.
>
> James 4:3 (CSB)

I knew better than to ask Dad to give me a car. I could have a car when I could pay for it and pay for the insurance. The cost of insurance for a young man seemed astronomical, much more than the price of a car. Dad knew handling the responsibility of a car myself would be good for me.

God is a generous father, but he won't give me something dangerous. He knows my motives. He won't give me something I intend to sin with. Sin is the most dangerous thing of all. The heavenly Father will give me the Holy Spirit.[19] He will help me cleanse my life from sin.

> PRAYER: Lord, thank you for all the good things you give me, especially for giving me the Holy Spirit. Amen.

PERSONAL THOUGHTS

---

[19]Luke 11:11–13.

62 The world's friend

> You adulterous people! Don't you know that friendship with the world is hostility toward God? So whoever wants to be the friend of the world becomes the enemy of God.
>
> James 4:4 (CSB)

Many worldly people live in a college dorm. Sharing space with them is inescapable, but I didn't need to follow their worldly lifestyle. While living in the dorm, I did my best to follow Jesus' example.

Satan's kingdom is called the "world." A friend of the world approves of evil values and actions. A friend of the world joins the party that celebrates immorality and greed. A friend of the world believes he must go along to be accepted.

Jesus loved worldly people without sinning. Jesus associated with prostitutes and corrupt tax collectors without sinning.[20] He called them to leave Satan's domain and to enter his kingdom.

> PRAYER: Lord, living the kingdom-of-heaven lifestyle is more important to me than being accepted by worldly friends. Amen.

---

[20]Mark 2:15–17.

63   Envies intensely

> Or do you think it's without reason that
> the Scripture says: The spirit [of God]
> made to dwell in us envies intensely?
>
> James 4:5 (CSB)

My wife and I love to spend time together. We reluctantly do errands alone. We feel out of place at social events whenever the other is not there. We love to share jokes, photos, and stories with each other. We both are aware of God's presence as we talk throughout the day.

God is jealous for my attention. He loves me so much that he is offended when the world captivates my attention. The Holy Spirit who is within me wants to interact with me every day, not just for an hour on Sunday.

> PRAYER: Lord, you are the center of my attention while I go about my daily activities. Amen.

PERSONAL THOUGHTS

64 Grace to the humble

> But [God] gives greater grace. Therefore
> he says:
>
> > God resists the proud,
> > but gives grace to the humble.
>
> James 4:6 (CSB)

When the guys got together to play flag football, each captain picked his players from the group. The big strong guy was the captain of one team. Instead of picking the best athlete, he always asked the most clumsy guy to be on his team.

Which side am I on, the proud side or the humble side? Which side is God on? The arrogant think they have everything, so God resists them. The humble know they lack what they need, so God favors them and supplies their needs.

> PRAYER: Lord, help me to become more
> humble. I need your grace. Amen.

PERSONAL THOUGHTS

65   Resist the devil

> Therefore, submit to God.   Resist the
> devil, and he will flee from you.
>
> James 4:7 (CSB)

The hobby supply store had boxes with a wood-grain finish. They looked sturdy. I could use something like that. When I opened a box, I saw it was made of cardboard with a photo of wood glued to the outside. I decided not to buy any.

The influence of the devil, Satan, is obvious in many areas of life. He tempts; he deceives; he opposes whatever is right. Some people fall for his tricks and do whatever he says. I'm not buying what he offers. When I submit to God, I see death is the consequence of sin. When I speak the truth, deception is defeated. When I take a stand for what is right, evil is exposed. If I will resist the devil, I will see he is not as powerful as I thought.

> PRAYER: Lord, I submit to you in every area, so the devil won't influence me. Amen.

PERSONAL THOUGHTS

66   Draw near to God

Draw near to God, and he will draw near
to you. Cleanse your hands, sinners, and
purify your hearts, you double-minded.
James 4:8 (CSB)

My neighbor was walking her dog when I came out
to visit. Her dog kept his distance until I offered my
hand for a smell-check. After that, he came up close
and we became best friends.

When I consider the vastness of creation, it
seems God must be on the other side of the universe. But if I will turn away from sin and toward
God's righteousness, he will come close to me. He
knows how weak I am, but his loving mercy is
greater.

PRAYER: Lord, thank you for being close.
Amen.

PERSONAL THOUGHTS

67 Cleanse your hands

> Cleanse your hands, sinners, and purify your hearts, you double-minded. Be miserable and mourn and weep. Let your laughter be turned to mourning and your joy to gloom.
>
> James 4:8–9 (CSB)

When I was little, I thought I'd dig a hole to China in the yard. I didn't get very far, and Mom made me fill up the hole. When I came in, she insisted that I wash up. I had to promise never to dig a hole to China again.

Repentance never feels good. When I repent, I see the mess caused by my sin. I see the emptiness of sin's fun. I see the dirt on my hands and in my heart. Do I really have to change? Yes, I must!

PRAYER: Lord, I repent of my sin. Thank you for your mercy. Amen.

PERSONAL THOUGHTS

68   Humbling myself

> Humble yourselves before the Lord, and
> he will exalt you.
>
> James 4:10 (CSB)

I was arrogant about my technical knowledge.
When a coworker was promoted instead of me, I re-
pented and told her I would do all I could to make
her successful, which I did. God used this event to
move me toward a new career a year later.

I knew I had a sin problem, and my technical
knowledge couldn't solve this problem. I know
God's forgiveness is the solution, and I must come
to him with a humble attitude. He will forgive.
With practice, humility is becoming a lifestyle.

> PRAYER: Lord, thank you for your for-
> giveness of my sin. Help me lay down
> my pride. Amen.

PERSONAL THOUGHTS

69 Criticizing

> Don't criticize one another, brothers and
> sisters. Anyone who defames or judges
> a fellow believer defames and judges the
> law. If you judge the law, you are not a
> doer of the law but a judge.
>
> James 4:11 (CSB)

My wife and I had friendships with a cluster of
home Bible study groups. We were unhappy when
the church leadership reorganized the clusters. It
was an excellent opportunity to criticize, but we
had read this verse in James' letter.

I don't have the right to criticize or judge another believer, as if I was a morality judge. I'm
not an expert on Christian dos and don'ts. I don't
know the motivations of others. I can recognize
some kinds of sin, but I am not a judge to condemn
anyone.

> PRAYER: Lord, even though I may be
> unhappy with how things are going,
> I will refuse to criticize your children.
> Amen.

PERSONAL THOUGHTS

70   The judge

> There is one lawgiver and judge who is
> able to save and to destroy. But who are
> you to judge your neighbor?
>
> James 4:12 (CSB)

A new believer and I had one-on-one Bible studies
for a while. I had to remind myself that he was also
a disciple of Jesus just like me. I was not qualified to
judge his mistakes. I had to be an example to him,
rather than a judge.

Only God is qualified to pass eternal judgment
on people. Through Jesus, he provided a way for
sins to be forgiven. Those who remain rebellious
will be destroyed. I can't usurp God's authority.

> PRAYER: Lord, I must admit I'm not
> qualified to judge others. Forgive me
> when I fall into a judgmental attitude.
> Amen.

PERSONAL THOUGHTS

71 Tomorrow

> Come now, you who say, "Today or to-
> morrow we will travel to such and such
> a city and spend a year there and do
> business and make a profit." Yet you do
> not know what tomorrow will bring—
> what your life will be!
>
> James 4:13–14 (CSB)

We had a reservation at a fancy restaurant for
Thanksgiving dinner with Ron and Betty. Then the
night before, we got a call. Ron was in the hospi-
tal. Even though his heart-attack symptoms had
abated, they wouldn't let him out. So, Betty joined
us for dinner and we visited Ron afterward.

Life is uncertain. I don't know what unexpected
event will upset my plans for tomorrow. It is arrogant for me to talk as if I'm in control of my future. I
may make plans and have good intentions, but they
must be tempered by the fact life is uncertain.

PRAYER: Lord, I must trust you for
whatever tomorrow may bring. Amen.

PERSONAL THOUGHTS

72   Smoke

> Yet you do not know what tomorrow will bring—what your life will be! For you are like vapor that appears for a little while, then vanishes.
>
> James 4:14 (CSB)

When we got the campfire lit, the flames and smoke went up into the sky and disappeared. The fire warmed us for a couple of hours but was cold by morning.

Like smoke from a fire, life on earth is temporary. My lifespan is short compared to the sweep of history. I don't know how long I have. I can't make solid plans for tomorrow. I must just live today. The best way to live today is following Jesus.

> PRAYER: Lord, I don't know what will happen tomorrow, but you do, so I will obey you today. Amen.

PERSONAL THOUGHTS

73   If the Lord wills

> Instead, you should say, "If the Lord wills, we will live and do this or that."
>
> James 4:15 (CSB)

I carefully planned the drive from Florida to Alabama. The trip was going well until we hit a traffic jam approaching Atlanta. I decided to take some back roads. We saw some lovely countryside and quaint small towns, but my detour added three hours to the trip. Maybe I wasn't such a good planner.

The events of my life are submitted to the will of God. He is sovereign over all the uncertainties of my life. The Holy Spirit nudges me to do things I didn't plan the day before.

> PRAYER: Lord, instead of pretending I'm in control, I will just do whatever you want. Amen.

PERSONAL THOUGHTS

74   Boasting

> But as it is, you boast in your arrogance.
> All such boasting is evil.
>
> James 4:16 (CSB)

Football fans from archrivals were having lunch together. Everyone in the restaurant could hear them. "My team is going to whup your team tomorrow!"

Boasting is merely my arrogance flowing from my heart out of my mouth. Thinking I can control my life tomorrow is usurping the authority of the king of the universe.

> PRAYER: Lord, I will repent of my pride whenever I hear myself boasting about tomorrow. Amen.

PERSONAL THOUGHTS

75   Knowing to do good

> So it is sin to know the good and yet not do it.
>
> James 4:17 (CSB)

My friend needed help painting his daughter's house. I didn't want to do it, but the Holy Spirit convinced me I should. I worked all Saturday morning with several other guys and we got much of it done. I didn't fall into the selfishness trap.

Opportunities to do good often pop up as surprises. If I'm preoccupied with my plans and selfish desires, I'll miss seeing someone in need who crosses my path. The Holy Spirit has many surprises for me if I will listen to him throughout the day. It is sin to ignore opportunities for good that I see.

PRAYER: Lord, help me recognize opportunities to do good. Amen.

PERSONAL THOUGHTS

76   Weeping over losses

> Come now, you rich people, weep and wail over the miseries that are coming on you.
>
> James 5:1 (CSB)

Enron Corporation was a major electricity, natural gas, communications, and pulp and paper company until its bankruptcy in 2001. I've met people who lost their jobs when the company closed down. The corporate leaders were convicted of institutionalized systematic accounting fraud and insider stock-market trading.

In this and the next few verses, James spoke against the rich who oppress others. They may think riches can buy a safe haven, but the Lord's judgment will bring misery, so there will be mourning over their losses.

PRAYER: Lord, you are the righteous judge. Nothing escapes your notice. Amen.

PERSONAL THOUGHTS

77   Rotted

> Your wealth has rotted and your clothes
> are moth-eaten. Your gold and silver are
> corroded, and their corrosion will be a
> witness against you and will eat your
> flesh like fire. You have stored up trea-
> sure in the last days.
>
> James 5:2–3 (CSB)

I went to an estate sale in a big warehouse, looking for a dining room table and chairs. The possessions of a deceased wealthy person were auctioned
to the highest bidders. The furniture and dishes
sold at bargain prices. Clothes that weren't moth-
eaten were given to a charity's thrift store. By the
end of the evening, the accumulated wealth of a
lifetime was gone.

In these verses, James continued to speak
against the corruption of the wealthy. One of their
crimes was to hoard their wealth instead of being
generous. The hoarding had gone on so long that
expensive garments in storage were moth-eaten
and metals were corroded and tarnished. Their
wealth will be ruined. Their health consumed like
a fire consumes a log.

> PRAYER: Lord, I repent of hoarding
> things for a "rainy day" instead of be-
> ing generous with what you have given
> me. Amen.

78 Cheating

> Look! The pay that you withheld from
> the workers who mowed your fields
> cries out, and the outcry of the har-
> vesters has reached the ears of the Lord
> of Hosts.
>
> James 5:4 (CSB)

The painters worked hard to finish the new house
next door to ours. At the end of the week, they were
sitting at the house waiting for the boss to come pay
them. After many complaints, eventually they were
paid.

James continued his condemnation of the corrupt rich. He listed three sins in this passage. This
verse explains the first, namely, cheating his workers out of their wages. The Lord guarantees justice
to the victims of evil men. The Lord is almighty at
the head of the armies of heaven. No rich man can
resist the Lord.

> PRAYER: Lord, I pray for speedy jus-
> tice for those oppressed by greedy men.
> Amen.

PERSONAL THOUGHTS

79   Living luxuriously

> You have lived luxuriously on the earth
> and have indulged yourselves. You
> have fattened your hearts in a day of
> slaughter.
>
> James 5:5 (CSB)

The real estate advertisement said one could buy a huge estate home in Southern California for only a few million dollars. It was once the luxurious home of a Hollywood mogul. The fine print of the advertisement said renovations would cost about one and a half million dollars. What had been a mansion was just a crumbling shell.

James continued his condemnation of the corrupt rich. Their second sin was a selfish lifestyle, living in luxury while cheating the workers. Their selfishness was just preparation for God's judgment. The corrupt have no concept of stewardship of the bounty God gives.[21]

> PRAYER: Lord, help me be a faithful steward of what you have given me. Amen.

PERSONAL THOUGHTS

---

[21] 1 Peter 4:10.

80   Condemning

> You have condemned, you have murdered the righteous, who does not resist you.
>
> James 5:6 (CSB)

Anthony Ray Hinton was held on Alabama's death row for 28 years after being wrongly convicted of two murders on flimsy evidence. He was exonerated in 2015 by the Supreme Court of the United States. He is the author of the memoir, *The Sun Does Shine: How I Found Life and Freedom on Death Row* (2018).

James completed his condemnation of the corrupt rich. This third sin was condemnation of the righteous, and even murder. The death penalty in a corrupt court is equivalent to murder. God's judgment will take its course.

PRAYER: Lord, help me to stand for justice whenever I serve on a jury. Amen.

PERSONAL THOUGHTS

81   Patience

> Therefore, brothers and sisters, be patient until the Lord's coming. See how the farmer waits for the precious fruit of the earth and is patient with it until it receives the early and the late rains.
>
> James 5:7 (CSB)

I ordered some furniture. When I went back to arrange for delivery, the store was gone and the phone wouldn't take messages. I was wishing Jesus would come back and give me justice. Oh, when Jesus returns, I won't need furniture. Never mind.

Even though the world is a mess and the corrupt get richer and richer, James said be patient for Jesus is coming again. His coming is guaranteed. He will bring justice to the earth. He will come when the Father determines that the time is right.

> PRAYER: Lord, I forgive those who have cheated me. Help me be patient, waiting for your coming. Amen.

PERSONAL THOUGHTS

82 Near

> You also must be patient. Strengthen your hearts, because the Lord's coming is near.
>
> James 5:8 (CSB)

When I was a kid, I had an advent calendar. I opened a little window on each day leading up to Christmas. Each window revealed a little picture. I was eager for Christmas to arrive, but the calendar showed me it was near but not yet.

I must be patient, waiting for the Lord's return. His coming is guaranteed. The Lord knows about all the difficulties I face in life. I can overcome them by the strength God gives me. I have a positive attitude, because I know the Lord's coming is near.

> PRAYER: Lord, thank you for the strength to overcome life's problems while I'm waiting for your coming. Amen.

PERSONAL THOUGHTS

83   Do not complain

> Brothers and sisters, do not complain about one another, so that you will not be judged. Look, the judge stands at the door!
>
> James 5:9 (CSB)

I was driving down the road, minding my own business, when this crazy guy zoomed past me and slammed on his brakes at the next stop light. I let everyone in my car know what I thought of him. Oops! I guess I was complaining.

James reminded me about Jesus' teaching, "Do not judge."[22] Complaining is the same as judging. Gossiping defiles the listener. God will judge me if I complain about others, because I usurp his authority.

> PRAYER: Lord, help me silence my complaining, because your return is near. Amen.

PERSONAL THOUGHTS

---

[22]Matthew 7:1–5.

84 Job

> Brothers and sisters, take the prophets who spoke in the Lord's name as an example of suffering and patience. See, we count as blessed those who have endured. You have heard of Job's endurance and have seen the outcome that the Lord brought about—the Lord is compassionate and merciful.
>
> James 5:10–11 (CSB)

Mike joined a running club to get some exercise. He won a lottery to get a place in the Chicago Marathon. He endured to the end. If I was to try a marathon, I'm sure Mike would have to carry me after the first couple of miles.

Job suffered in his body and suffered socially when his friends accused him, but God exonerated him.[23] My trials are not near as severe as Job's. If God gave him strength to endure, he will give me strength, too.

> PRAYER: Lord, you are compassionate and merciful. Thank you for giving me strength to endure my trials. Amen.

---

[23]Job 42:7.

85 Oaths

> Above all, my brothers and sisters, do not swear, either by heaven or by earth or with any other oath. But let your "yes" mean "yes," and your "no" mean "no," so that you won't fall under judgment.
>
> James 5:12 (CSB)

I asked Mom, "Can I have a cookie?" She said, "No." Five minutes later I asked, "May I have a cookie now?" I learned at a young age she meant what she said. I would just get in trouble if I pestered her. Negotiation would go nowhere.

James reminded us of Jesus' teaching about oaths.[24] My speech must be consistent. When I say "Yes" or "No," it must always mean just that. I don't need to swear to convince listeners I mean what I say.

> PRAYER: Lord, help me be consistent in what I say, never waffling. Amen.

PERSONAL THOUGHTS

---

[24]Matthew 5:33–37.

86   Suffering or cheerful

> Is anyone among you suffering? He
> should pray. Is anyone cheerful? He
> should sing praises.
>
> James 5:13 (CSB)

The church calendar had two events on Saturday. A funeral was scheduled for the morning and a wedding for the afternoon. The church family was both grieving over the loss of a brother and rejoicing over the love of the couple.

James pointed out two occasions for prayer: petitions when suffering and praise when cheerful. Life runs on two parallel tracks: sorrow and rejoicing. While I'm suffering and petitioning, someone else is cheerful and praising. Later the situations are reversed.

> PRAYER: Lord, no matter the circumstances, I will pray. I will ask for your grace, and I will praise you for your love and mercy. Amen.

PERSONAL THOUGHTS

87   Prayer for the sick

> Is anyone among you sick? He should
> call for the elders of the church, and they
> are to pray over him, anointing him with
> oil in the name of the Lord. The prayer
> of faith will save the sick person, and the
> Lord will raise him up.
>
> James 5:14–15 (CSB)

Meredith was diagnosed with Stage IV cancer in
her lung. The elders of my church prayed. The
whole church prayed. A wide circle of friends prayed. After participating in an experimental clinical
trial, she was completely cancer-free. She was still
cancer-free more than three years later. On average,
people with this type of cancer die within fourteen
months of diagnosis.

James explained that prayer for the sick will be
effective. Prayer is not just pious words. Prayer
is not shouting or weeping. Prayer is not a certain
posture. Prayer is a conversation with God based
on faith. Prayer for the sick is an honest humble
request to our Lord who promised to respond.

> PRAYER: Lord, I will pray persistently
> for those who are sick. Amen.

PERSONAL THOUGHTS

88 Confession

> If [the sick person] has committed sins, he will be forgiven. Therefore, confess your sins to one another and pray for one another, so that you may be healed.
>
> James 5:15–16 (CSB)

Healthy relationships with other Christians require honesty about my sins and weaknesses. Confession and apologies are steps toward forgiveness. Prayer for one another is a step toward healing of diseases. I will be quick to apologize, so my brothers can sincerely pray for me. I will be quick to forgive offenses, so I can pray and see my brothers healed.

> PRAYER: Lord, I will be always ready to pray for my fellow believers, especially those who are sick. Amen.

PERSONAL THOUGHTS

89   Effective prayer

> The prayer of a righteous person is very powerful in its effect. Elijah was a human being as we are, and he prayed earnestly that it would not rain, and for three years and six months it did not rain on the land. Then he prayed again, and the sky gave rain and the land produced its fruit.
>
> James 5:16–18 (CSB)

The little girl in the grocery aisle was tugging on Mom's slacks. When a child has an urgent request, a wise parent pays attention to the child. A parent must be ready for interruptions.

Elijah is an example of a man who prayed effectively.[25] Because of the pagan leadership of the king of Israel, he prayed for the rains to stop. After a confrontation with the prophets of Baal, he prayed and the rains resumed. Elijah was an ordinary guy like me. After my sins are forgiven, I will be ready for effective prayer.

> PRAYER: Lord, thank you for loving your children and answering my prayers. Amen.

---

[25]1 Kings 17:1–18:45.

90 Turning a sinner

My brothers and sisters, if any among
you strays from the truth, and someone
turns him back, let that person know
that whoever turns a sinner from the er-
ror of his way will save his soul from
death and cover a multitude of sins.

James 5:19–20 (CSB)

Angie says she grew up as a "heathen." Her mother
was radically changed when she was saved as an
adult. Angie talked on the phone with her mother
about a fungus on her dog's nose that wouldn't
heal. Angie's mother prayed for the dog right then,
and he was healed. That opened Angie's eyes to the
gospel.

Remaining in sin, refusing the truth, and re-
belling against God has deadly consequences.
Turning such a person toward the grace of God is
worth the heart-ache, effort, and prayer.

PRAYER: Lord, give me the right words
to say to those who stray from your
truth. Amen.

Index

About the author

Edward B. Allen is the author of books for three styles of devotional Bible study. Verse-by-verse books draw devotional points from the Scripture passage in sequence. Historical-people books focus on incidents in the lives of historical people that illustrate biblical principles. Topical books explore relevant Scriptures throughout the Bible. His books also include many personal stories from modern life.

His books are in two series. Books in the *A Slow Walk* series have short meditations in daily-devotional format, such as *A Slow Walk through Psalm 119: 90 Devotional Meditations*. Books in the *Devotional Commentary* series are straight reads with a devotional slant, rather than academic or theological comments, such as *Practical Faith: A Devotional Commentary*.

He has led discussion Bible-study groups in evangelical churches for over 50 years He received a Ph.D. in Computer Science degree at Florida Atlantic University and had a career in software engineering. He has authored or coauthored over 80 professional papers.

www.ingramcontent.com/pod-product-compliance
Lightning Source LLC
Chambersburg PA
CBHW071815020426
42331CB00007B/1488